# AS I REMEMBER IT ALL

T0208420

# As I Remember It All

CHARLES D. STATTON

iUniverse, Inc.
New York  Bloomington

# As I Remember It All

iUniverse books may be ordered through booksellers or by contacting:

iUniverse
1663 Liberty Drive
Bloomington, IN 47403
www.iuniverse.com
1-800-Authors (1-800-288-4677)

ISBN: 978-1-4502-0836-9 (pbk)
ISBN: 978-1-4502-0837-6 (ebook)

Printed in the United States of America

iUniverse rev. date: 2/25/10

# AS I REMEMBER IT ALL

By Charles D. Statton

My earliest memories of family life probably began at age four. We lived in the town of Boone, Iowa, with a population of about ten thousand, which was a central maintenance facility for the C&NW Railroad where my dad started as an apprentice machinist and was elevated to a full status machinist. Many men worked at the Maintenance Center, as this was the largest employer in Boone and home base for engineers, fireman, conductors, and brakemen. Dad walked to and from work every weekday, his work was only about four blocks from home, carrying a lunch pail which Mom

had packed with a filled coffee thermos, sandwiches, and desserts.

Dad made a lot of friends on the job and as they ate lunch together they would talk about their families and their plans for the future. Some of his friends were not married and lived in boarding houses. One of Dad's supervisors was Mr. Louis Weinsberger, the father of Doris Weinsberger a classmate of mine all through school. Throughout these years I visited, along with other friends, Doris's home and met her mother, Frida. They were a fully Swiss family and demanded strict house and conduct rules. Louis, Doris's father, made his own wine and we were not to consume any of it.

I recall that my father bought a four-bedroom house on Seventh Street in Boone, hired a contractor to raise the structure on heavy timbers and dig out a basement. They poured a concrete floor in the basement, tiled the walls, installed a central heating system, and lowered the house to close it all. My father had our home connected to the city's central sewage and water system, as well as the electric and

gas companies. To me it was an amazing example of my dad's ability and dedication to family life, as well as of his great ambitions and talent.

To a small boy the basement seemed large. It had a laundry room and space where my mom could hang laundry in the winter to dry. It also included a workshop for my dad, a coal bin to hold furnace fuel, and space to store the fruit and jams my mother canned in the summer for our family's winter consumption. I learned a lot in the workshop when my dad built an ice box for food storage with a block-ice compartment. We did not own a refrigerator

The house had a great screened-in porch, and we would plead with Mom to let us sleep on the porch on those warm summer night. She would have us first clean the floor with soap and water. Then when it was dry we could put our blankets and pillows on the floor. It was worth all the effort and we did that frequently during the summer. We would leave the door to the living room open to listen to the radio.

My older brother Steve and my sister Ila were our family then; my brother Dan was born a year later.

We had the first radio in the neighborhood, an Atwater Kent unit. After school, we would listen to programs such as *Little Orphan Annie,* with Daddy Warbucks; *Jack Armstrong, the All-American Boy; The Air Adventures of Jimmy Allen,* and others.

Some programs would end with coded messages and we could get a decoder button by sending in a box top from Wheaties, Ovaltine, or other kids' products. We would form clubs and the neighbor children would join with us as we decoded messages. What a life we had, with full space for imagination. Life was totally interesting and educational.

Dad and Mom liked the radio programs *Amos & Andy, The Eddie Cantor Show, Jack Benny,* and the summer ball games announced by "Dutch" Reagan (President Ronald Reagan, years later) over radio station WHO from Des Moines, Iowa. As children we also listened to scary programs like *The Shadow,* and *The Ghost of Lake Tapaho*

My older brother listened to opera, which the Texaco Oil Company sponsored on Saturday afternoon. On Saturday evening we listened to The Grand Ol' Opry. All in all it was a special time in family life, and as children we were assigned each evening to wash the dishes, dry them, and put them away.

In the evenings of our early years Mother would read to us from Mother Westwind about the merry little breezes—Brer Rabbit, Rumpelstiltskin, and others. She felt that we all needed library cards and should do a lot of reading, and we all did so.

A neighborhood grocer was a couple of blocks from our house where, on weekends, we could buy things that Mom was out of, like butter, eggs, or cereal. Most of the time, however, our groceries were purchased downtown, and home delivered, from John Austin Grocery. On Dad's payday Mom would go downtown and pay our bill. John would usually give us a bag with the bills in it, and a candy bar that Mom would cut in pieces for all of us children. My

mother's hairdresser, Mrs. Finley, lived near us and Mom's hair appointments were Friday mornings.

Two things were required when we started school: we had to bring a card from our dentist (Dr. Barth) stating that he had checked our teeth; we also had to get reports from our doctor that we had gotten vaccination shots.

By 1929 the Depression hit everyone hard. My dad was laid off from C&NW Railroad where he was a fulltime machinist on the railway system. I recall that my dad "bumped" a position to Clinton, Iowa, on C&NW railroad. So we all went to Clinton to live, but only for a short period, then that position was eliminated. My dad's heart and spirit broke, and we returned to Boone. After awhile Mom and Dad decided to leave Boone and go to California. We had a sale of all our household furniture, kitchenware, radio, and everything we owned and Dad arranged for us to travel by train, as a family, to California where we would live with Dad's biological mother. My mom was just then pregnant

with Ed and trying to survive whooping cough. Except for the farmers, the town of Boone was dead.

Before we left Mom had Johnstones' Bakery bake us a ham and we brought that, along with a basket of fruit, on the train to feed all of us for lunch. For breakfast we would eat oranges and milk that Mom bought. I don't remember how we did dinner. We had a bedroom in the sleeper car. The conductor would make up the beds each night and help us in. I think I slept with Dan; Steve with Dad; my sister Ila with Mom. Wherever the train had to stop for fuel and water for the engine, the station had a franchised restaurant.

After some five days we arrived in Los Angeles and were met by Dad's biological mother. We traveled by car to the "Sunset Golf Course" where my grandmother and her husband, George Gotlieb, lived. George was the caretaker and night watchman.

I loved walking to the gate in the evening with my new grandfather to close the gate. On the days when school was out my brothers Steve and Dan and sister Ila and I would

walk up the hill that was full of poppies and overlooked a police shooting range.

On weekend Saturdays my grandmother would fix a picnic basket and take us to Santa Monica beach. To an Iowa family, nothing could be better.

My grandmother was very religious, and every Sunday morning she would pray with us, then off we would go to the Foursquare Gospel Church where Aimee Semple McPherson was the minister. We attended Sunday school, then church services, church lunch, and spent the remaining day on the church grounds before returning home after the evening services. My grandmother played trumpet in the church orchestra. She was totally absorbed by Aimee and gave far too much of George's assets to the church. George never went to church. One Sunday, after one of Aimee's sermons to the Sunday school class, Grandmother had me sign a pledge that I would never smoke. She was a real spiritual influence on me. I used to be able to recite all the books in the Bible in proper order.

My grandmother drove us to Burbank to school during the week. It was the 42nd Street School. Then she would pick us up after school and bring us back to her home on the golf course. Her car had a rumble seat, and we took turns riding in it because it would seat only two people.

In the summer we stayed at my aunt and uncle's ranch south of Fresno, California, where Dad was helping my uncle build a house. I particularly loved my experience there. As children we had a lot of freedom. We were allowed to build tree houses in the nearby eucalyptus trees. Walter Bonitz, my uncle, was from a German family that owned the Alexander Hotel in Los Angeles; however, he wanted to experience ranch life rather than city life. He raised chickens—roosters and laying hens. He would collect the fertilized eggs and put them in his electric incubator to hatch. He also had grapes that were grown for raisins. Sun-Maid would come to the ranch to package the raisins. As children we collected raisins in chili bottles. I learned a lot about ranch life from the hired

hands. I also learned how to use bad language. What a time for developing minds!

The housekeeper had a boyfriend who would come and visit her. My Uncle Walter did not like him and, particularly when he had a little too much to drink and his German temper was at its peak, he would threaten to shoot him. It was always a dramatic evening affair when all that occurred.

Once he bought a prize bull at an auction in Fresno. His intention was to use him to breed cattle. However, one time my uncle's son went into the bullpen and the bull gored him. After getting his son to the hospital Walter returned to the ranch, got his rifle, and killed the bull.

During our stay we would sometimes see clouds of dust from sheepherders crossing the area. Uncle Walter would not allow them to cross his land where grapes and cotton were growing. His dramatic behavior was often difficult for my Aunt Birdella, my father's sister.

When the house was well underway, Dad and Mom decided to drive back to Iowa in caravan with my dad's sister

and Uncle Dave and their two children, Warren and Helen. The trip home was tedious but eventful for us children. We saw a lot of the country, including the Petrified Forest. Uncle Dave carried a revolver in the car as his form of security.

Soon after we returned to Boone, Iowa, in 1930, my younger brother Ed was born. Dad rented a house on Fifth Street and we older children started back to school. Dad had a job with the Holland Furnace Company, installing furnaces and operating cleaning systems. Dad bought his first car with a World War I soldier's bonus check. Dad regained his ambition, but he never again trusted the banks or big business.

I recall our first family driving vacation in Dad's seven-passenger Buick Touring Car with three spare tires and a rear trunk. Before we left town Dad had the car checked, gassed, and greased at the garage my Uncle Dave's brother operated.

We left early in the morning and drove from Boone to Brookfield, Missouri, where my mother's adopted family

lived in a house that was large to my eyes. The adopted grandfather, along with a partner, owned and operated a deep-shaft coal mine. The two half-brothers drove a truck route delivering soda pop and Coca Cola. Occasionally we got a bottle of pop.

My grandmother showed me how to make butter in a churn. We enjoyed our short stay before driving back home to Boone.

Democrat Franklin Delano Roosevelt was elected president of the United States in 1932, and Dad was an ardent Democrat and follower. My brother Dan picked up the banner later in life as a lawyer in our hometown of Boone.

Dad had a lot more drive than he exhibited at home. His idea was to get each of us on in life; Dad was the disciplinarian. Mom's idea was that the motives we held and the talents we had would be used to help us succeed.

I don't remember ever dwelling on how our family had to scrape by on little during the Great Depression.

Most of my neighbors and school friends were in similar circumstances. As children we made all of our own birthday and Christmas cards. We made "May baskets," and colored boiled eggs at Easter. Sometimes our clothes were hand-me-downs. At Christmas Mom would take us to the C&NW Railroad Ladies' Club for "goodies." Mom belonged to a church ladies' circle.

I remember going Christmas shopping with my brother Dan, spending what money I earned from my magazine route. I delivered *Country Gentlemen, Ladies' Home Journal, Liberty* magazines, and others. Dan and I bought each other pocket knives for Christmas. I remember getting my dad a tin of Flat Fifties, already-rolled cigarettes, for Christmas. My dad rolled his own cigarettes from a bag of Bull Durham tobacco and a sheet from his book of cigarette papers, as most smokers did. Later on he switched to manufactured and boxed cigarettes. He seldom, if ever, smoked cigars like my Uncle Dave.

Our family food menus seldom varied, except in summer when apples, rhubarb, corn, pears, and cherries were available for canning and meal preparation. Saturday night was bean soup or Boston style baked beans; Sunday, Swiss steak, etc. Mom usually spent most Saturdays baking pies, cakes, bread, and cinnamon rolls. Later in the day it was my duty to carry a basket of fresh-baked goods to our Aunt Cindy, a few blocks away. Mom loved to help others as best she could after our family needs were met.

All of these family adventures left me with a strong sense of creativity, generosity, self-reliance, and self-esteem that has endured throughout my entire life.

In the early years on 7th Street, and I don't remember the actual date, but the County Health Department found scarlet fever in our home. (Dr. Healy had to report it.) I was afflicted the worst; my sister Ila came down similarly, then Dan, but with a much milder case. A large yellow tag was nailed to the door. Mom cooled my fever with cold cloths and cool soda water baths. I recovered slowly.

My dad was cleared and he moved in with Aunt Cindy so that he could continue working. He came by the house daily and talked to us from the front sidewalk. Dr. Healy came several times a week. I don't recall if my brother Steve stayed at the house or left with Dad.

We remained house quarantined for several weeks before the sign was taken down. My dad must have brought the food my mom needed. Our home had to be closed and fumigated by burning formaldehyde candles in the rooms when we all recovered, again as a health department decree.

The suspect carrier in all this was the dairy milk that was delivered daily; it was non-pasteurized and Todd's dairy was shut down, forced to close.

Our County Health Department had to solve their own problems. There was no U.S. Center for Disease Control. Most of the meat products in our local markets came from local butchers that were not subject to inspection. Fortunately, the population endured and survived.

Our grade school was close to home and we walked to Bryant School. My teacher was Miss Holmes, and she was a stickler for proper conduct and class participation. My classmates were special to me and we participated together at recess in regular sports.

Our school janitor liked me and would hire me for Saturday morning cleanup, carrying ashes out from the furnace, sweeping, and other tasks. I earned enough money for Saturday afternoon movies, which cost five to ten cents.

The classmates I recall were Bob Lamb, his cousin Dan Lamb, Doris Weinsberger, and Wyoma Iden.

I had my first lecture on the sexual differences between boys and girls, as well as proper sexual behavior, at Wyoma's home. Her mother gave us all the details while we sat on their porch. Wyoma's mother was a single mom. Those lessons, coupled with my dad's strict behavior discipline, lasted in me forever.

One Sunday afternoon (December 7, 1941) I heard President Roosevelt announce the attack on Pearl Harbor.

My mom and dad were there to hear it all. I knew what I wanted to do in this pending war, as I had nearly completed my training for a pilot's license.

I had some great instructors in high school and their images still remain in my memory bank. Doctor Cunningham, my physics instructor, inspired me. I earned great marks but he would tell me that my brother Steve was much better. I was good at math, chemistry, and workshop where I learned to do cabinet work, cut and polish metal, and cast moldings. I doubt if workshop classes exist in today's education systems.

We had great coaches in sports: Coach Wayne Hill in football, and Coach Bucky O'Conner in basketball, who later was chosen to coach basketball at the University of Iowa.

Our language instructors were good, but it was hard for me to judge since I earned modest grades in both Spanish and Latin.

Our weekend entertainment during my high school years was during the era of the big-band one-night stands. We would hitchhike or go with somebody's parent driving to

the ballroom in Des Moines (about forty miles from home). We heard and watched Glen Miller, Woody Herman, Tommy Dorsey, Benny Goodman, and others. It was inexpensive and excellent entertainment. We didn't miss any opportunity in Des Moines, and we purchased their records and would play them in a rented hall in Boone for our own high school dances in the winter. It was a great and creative time for us.

Our high school graduation class of 1942 was destined to grow in those times. A good many went on to college. Every five years, as long as we were able, we celebrated a class reunion. I was proud to be among them and attended a great number of reunions. All in all it was a great group of what Tom Brokaw called The Greatest Generation.

I had to work if I wanted to go to college. My parents could not help us as they gave all they earned to keep our family going, and I didn't see that they were obligated to send me to college. I worked in John Austin's Grocery, and also at Peterson's Clothing Store. It was a great time of education for

me as I saw what other people in town ordered for food and how they bought their clothes.

One customer at the clothing store would come in and buy a suit or coat. Our store owner, Duke Peterson, was always impeccably dressed—suit, vest, tie. This particular customer would come in and say that he was looking for a suit to knock around in, "something like what Duke had on." It always brought a lot of laughs.

A school classmate, as well as from our Sunday school class, Marv Elverts also worked at Peterson's Clothing Store. A girl I often dated, Mary Lou Doyle, a Catholic, would pass by our clothing store on her way to Saturday morning confession at the church. My clothing store co-worker would go out front and encourage Mary Lou not to confess what she and I did on dates. Her mother was often with her and I would be totally consumed in embarrassment at Marv's fun time, although he never knew anything other than I occasionally dated Mary Lou. Our next date would be rather "cool" until I could explain it all as Marv's idea of fun.

At the clothing store Duke Peterson would measure and mark changes needed on purchased clothing and I would walk them down to the tailor shop for modifications and pressing. Then I would pick them up and bring them back to the store.

The partner and manager of the store, Fred Schmidt, would joke with us about business practices. He said he kept two sets of accounting books, one set he called "fire books," which carried inventory at much higher cost levels in case of fire. The other set seemed to keep the honest levels of inventory. Although we joked about the practice, I was never sure that many businesses were not using such practice.

Over the summer, after buying too many employee discount clothes for myself, I managed to save $125 for my first year in college at Cedar Falls, Iowa, Four other students from my high school also attended school in Cedar Falls and we shared an apartment in Waterloo and rode the bus to Cedar Falls for classes. I bought a meal card at a local restaurant. Each time I used it the charges would be punched

out on the card. I found an evening job (5:00 to midnight), first at a machine shop and later at a bakery, loading delivery trucks; the hours were about the same.

It was at Cedar Falls that I first met Marilynn Camp who later became my marriage partner. We met at a dance at "Spider Webbs" dance pavilion in Waterloo, Iowa. We seemed right for each other and continued dating until I left school for Air Force training. We were engaged to marry before I left for service in China, Burma, and India. We corresponded by mail via my military APO address in China. I recall how great it was to go to mail call once a week to get my mail from Marilynn and my mom. My dad seldom wrote.

I survived financially in school, in part, by sending my laundry home by bus to my mom who would do all the work, pack it up and return it by bus to me. Often she would include home-baked cookies or some cash. It all worked for me.

During high school my brother Steve had a job delivering milk by horse and buggy in the early mornings,

and later had a job in an ice cream parlor. And I had a job carrying newspapers, the *Des Moines Register* and *Tribune*, in the early mornings. It was difficult in winter as we started at 4:00 A.M.

Delivering papers was an early education in business practices and consumer habits. Our manager would hold "route meetings" on Thursday evenings at 7:00. We were sent out into our delivery neighborhoods and had to report back by 9:00with results of our search for new customers. The manager would ask, 'How many homes did you call on?" And, "How many did you get inside of?" And finally, "How many 'starts' [new orders] did you get?" At week's end he would post the name of the route carrier who did the best. In the summer the manager would take us all to the Iowa State Fair for a day. We rode on our electric interurban train, the Fort Dodge, Des Moines and Southern. The rail line no longer exists.

I wanted to earn enough money for a bicycle and use it for delivery in good weather. I finally achieved my

goal, but abandoned my paper delivery job, as it was far too time consuming and earnings were meager. Collecting money from customers took Friday evenings and Saturday mornings. It was exhausting for small pay. Some customers would claim that someone must have stolen their deliveries all week; therefore, they would not pay me at all. Such consumer attitudes shocked me, but I had no alternative but to pay the manager for all customer orders. If it occurred more than once I canceled their orders.

After high school my brother Dan worked as a fireman on the C&NW Railroad's coal-fired locomotives to save money for school. The pay was excellent and he went to Drake University Law School.

Steve, after high school, went to Iowa State University to the school of chemical engineering and emerged as valedictorian of the graduating class. He then decided to go to medical school at the University of Iowa at Iowa City, from which he graduated.

My sister Ila worked in an arsenal facility in Ankaney, Iowa, commuting with other workers.

All of us older children earned our way into higher education, a real personal achievement for each of us. Our parents had given us all we needed during our at-home years and we gained from it all. They did not owe us further education.

I finished my first year at college and then was called up by the Army Air Corp, where I had applied earlier in the year. From then on it was all up to me to use and expose any of my talents; I thrived on the challenge and opportunity. I was good at flying and could fly multi-engine as well as single-engine fighter aircraft.

I don't remember the political affiliations of my brother Steve or sister Ila, but I was an ardent Republican (even though I voted for Harry Truman for president, and for Lyndon Johnson, John Kennedy's Vice President, when he ran for a second term after John Kennedy's assassination).

I was all for equal rights for "colored people" and could not buy Senator Goldwater's pronouncements.

At the time of the Goldwater/Johnson presidential run I was heading up a Bechtel East Coast design business, where we were designing a power facility for Potomac Electrical Power Company. The personnel facilities had to have separate lockers and washrooms for the "colored people." That seemed offensive to me, but was ancient tradition with the Potomac Electric Power Company.

The company also had two employee picnics in the summer—one for the Whites and one for the Blacks. I requested, and got, permission to attend the picnic for the Blacks as well as the one for the Whites.

While all of this seems out of order now, it had been a practice for businesses, railroads, restaurants, and travel for years, and was not about to be easily changed. However, after Martin Luther King's assassination in Memphis, Tennessee, President Johnson, by proclamation, put an end to segregation.

Our design office thrived on the East Coast and, over a period of eight years, we built up a team of twenty-five hundred engineers in the office and about fifty thousand in construction workers and field egineers. We ended up with more work for the new Bechtel East Coast office than we could handle and managed to annoy some new clients when we turned down invitations to bid their new projects. We became somewhat arrogant as Bechtel's East Coast presence was regarded as high prestige, where Bechtel had not been totally welcome at the beginning. Up until then, all the work was assigned to Stone & Webster, United Engineers, or to Ebasco. We moved into their territory with no welcome signs, and managed well. Our East Coast office achieved the status as a power division and I had my first election as vice president and later as director of the Bechtel Group.

Charles Statton

Appointed Vice Chairman of Bechtel's First Joint Venture in Taiwan With such a beginning and other life experiences, and the self-confidence I gained over the years, the real challenges now come with age and health disabilities I have to deal with daily. Losing my hearing, experiencing some balance problems (I am committed to a walker), and undergoing a heart operation demand that I keep physically fit with the help of a personal trainer, and my wife Linda's help with phone appointments, doctor visits, and limited travel.

Aging brings a whole new dimension into the long-established and usual methods of the past. The practices once followed now yield to current capability. Taking out and retrieving the trash cans, gardening, and leisure travel are curtailed to the capabilities that are destabilized by eyesight, balance, and lowered confidence, as well as loss of hearing ability.

Linda, my partner in life for the past twenty-seven years, and now my constant caregiver, is left to pick up all these duties, which now cause their own frustrations since she has a constant pain in her neck and shoulder. Learning to cope with it all is sometimes difficult and often unresolvable.

Linda now has to set up and schedule all the doctor appointments, and go with me as, oftentimes, I don't hear all the physicians have to tell me. Linda also organizes my prescription drug needs as well as all my daily vitamin supplements so that I am always assured of supply on time.

Linda takes care of all the laundry and leaves the housecleaning and ironing to our attendee. It all works for us.

Fortunately, I can still get to my physical training regularly and work with a personal trainer. That effort pays good dividends to my confidence in myself, even though I am committed to a walker, even in the gym, as well as a catheter, which has its drawbacks.

I am learning slowly the art of dealing with these disturbances without complaining and finding solutions that seem to fit my everyday life. I am committed to getting the most out of my remaining life, as I do enjoy what I have and the tasks I want to complete.

Both Linda and I spend a lot of time with my family gatherings at grandchildren marriages or family reunions. We visit with her two boys, Troy and Ty, both of whom are chefs, so the bulk of conversation centers on food, wine, etc. Since I am not in that league I do not participate in the enlarged discussions among these three gourmet experts.

Linda and I try to have lunch out each day and the choice of locations is usually based upon my ability to hear and the comfort of the chair or seat, as I no longer have much padding on my fanny. Also, restaurant access is a consideration for cane or walker entry.

It sounds like a lot of complaints, but it is all a reality that I am getting accustomed to and is becoming easier each day; and I vow to continue with grace.

Project Engineer & Author C.D. Statton,
Age 38
Bechtel's Beginning on the East Coast

Staff Member Making Blueprints at East Coast Office

First Engineers from Bechtel San Francisco
Get Project Going on East Coast

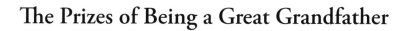
The Prizes of Being a Great Grandfather

Great Grandchild Allison, Age 18 months, 9/30/09

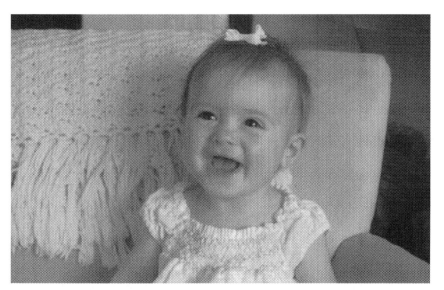

Great Grandchild Claire at 14 months, 9/30/09